Kids Jokes
Jokes For Kids
Book 1
Jackson Jones

Q: What do you give a sick bird?
A: Tweetment!

Q: What is a cat's favorite color?
A: Purrr-ple.

Q: what is a tree's favorite drink?
A: root beer!

Q: Which is the most talkative flower?
A: Tulip because it has two lips.

Q: what has four wheels and flies?
A: A garbage truck!

Q: Why couldn't the young pirate watch the movie?
A: Because it was rated ARRRRR.

Q: What did one egg say to the other egg?
A: You crack me up!

Q: Where do cars go for a swim?
A: At the carpool!

Q: What is a tornado's favorite game?
A: Twister!

Q: Why did the banana go to the doctor?
A: Because it wasn't peeling well.

Q: What type of music are balloons scared of?
A: Pop music!

Q: Why did the cookie go to the hospital?
A: He was feeling really crumby!

Q: What did the paper say to the pencil?
A: Write on!

Q: What did one wall say to the other wall?
A: I'll meet you at the corner.

Q: Why were the teacher's eyes crossed?
A: She couldn't control her pupils!

Q: What is the difference between a car and a bull?
A: A car only has one horn.

Q: Why do hummingbirds hum?
A: Because they don't know the words.

Q: What has hands but can not clap?
A: A clock!

Q: What does a witch use to keep her hair up?
A: Scarespray!

Q: Why did the boy put candy under his pillow?
A: Because he wanted sweet dreams.

Q. What has four legs but can't walk?
A. A table!

Q. Where do snowmen keep their money?
A. In snow banks.

Q. What did the water say to the boat?
A. Nothing, it just waved!

Q. Why didn't the chicken cross the road?
A. He was a chicken.

Q. What has one head, one foot and four legs?
A. A bed.

Q. What do sea monsters eat?
A. Fish and ships.

Q: Why did the orange stop in the middle of the hill?
A: It ran out of juice!

Q: What is the world's longest punctuation mark?
A: The hundred yard dash.

Q: How do you fix a broken vegetable?
A: With tomato paste.

Q: What do you call a fairy who doesn't take a bath?
A: Stinker Bell!

Q: What has three letters and starts with gas?
A: A car.

Q: What do a baker and a millionaire have in common?
A: They are both rolling in the dough!

Q: What did one flower say to the other flower?
A: Hey, bud!

Q: What's a royal pardon?
A: It's what the queen says after she burps.

Q: Why was 6 afraid of 7?
A: Because 7 ate 9.

Q: What goes on and on and has an "i" in the middle?
A: An onion.

Q: What kind of shoes do bananas make?
A: Slippers!

Q: What do you call a cow in a tornado?
A: A milkshake!

Q: What did the computer do at lunchtime?
A: Had a byte!

Q: What is an elephant's favorite sport?
A: Squash.

Q: What do you get if you cross fireworks with a duck?
A: A firequacker!

Q: What does a triceratops sit on?
A: Its tricera-bottom.

Q: What do you get when you cross a snowman with a vampire?
A: Frostbite.

Q: Who isn't hungry on Thanksgiving?
A: The turkey, because he's already stuffed!

Q: What kind of shorts do clouds wear?
A: Thunderwear!

Q: What goes up and down but does not move?
A: Stairs.

Q: Why do dragons sleep during the day?
A: So they can fight knights!

Q: Why can't your nose be 12 inches long?
A: Because then it would be a foot!

Q: What is full of holes but can still hold water?
A: A sponge!

Q: What stays in the corner, but travels around the world?
A: A stamp!

Q: Where do pencils come from?
A: Pencil-vania!

Q: Why was the math book sad?
A: Because it had too many problems.

Q: Why did the golfer wear two pairs of pants?
A: In case he got a hole in one!

Q: Where do mice park their boats?
A: At the hickory dickory dock.

Q: What kind of math do Snowy Owls like?
A: Owlgebra.

Q: What can you catch but not throw?
A: A cold.

Q: Why didn't the skeleton want to go to school?
A: His heart wasn't in it.

Q. What did the ground say to the earthquake?
A. You crack me up!

Q. What did the spider do on the computer?
A. Made a website!

Q. Why couldn't the pirate play cards?
A. Because he was sitting on the deck!

Q. What breaks when you say it?
A. Silence!

Q. What starts with a P, ends with an E, and has a million letters in it?
A. Post Office.

Q. Why can't a leopard hide?
A. Because he is always spotted.

Q. How do you make seven an even number?
A. You take the "s" off.

Q. What 3 inventions help man up in the world?
A. The elevator, the ladder, and the alarm clock.

Q. What kind of shoes do spies wear?
A. Sneakers.

Q. Why can't a bicycle stand up by itself?
A. Because it's two-tired.

Q: What nails do carpenters hate to hit?
A: Fingernails!

Q: What two things can you not have for breakfast?
A: Lunch and dinner.

Q: What is a boxer's favorite drink?
A: Punch!

Q: What did one hair say to the other?
A: It takes two to tangle!

Q: What did Tennessee?
A: The same thing Arkansas.

Q: Why did the banana split?
A: It saw the ginger snap.

Q: What can you hold without using your hands?
A: Your breath!

Q: What is the best time to go to the dentist?
A: Tooth-hurty.

Q: What kind of band can't play music?
A: A rubber band!

Q: How does a train sneeze?
A: Ah-choo-choo!

Q: What did the baby corn ask the mother corn?
A: Where is pop corn?

Q. What did the clock do after it ate?
A. It went back four seconds!

Q. What do you call a paleontologist who sleeps all the time?
A. Lazy bones.

Q: What did the cowboy say when his dog ran away?
A: Well, doggone!

Q: What time does a duck wake up?
A: At the quack of dawn!

Q: What time is it when an elephant sits on the fence?
A: Time to fix the fence!

Q: What did the horse say when it fell?
A: I've fallen and I can't giddy-up!

Q: What is a rabbit's favorite dance style?
A: Hip-Hop!

Q: Why did the computer keep sneezing?
A: It had a virus!

Q: What do you call cheese that isn't yours?
A: Nacho cheese!

Q: Why was the baby ghost sad?
A: He wanted his mummy!

Q: What makes pirates such good singers?
A: They can hit the high Cs.

Q: What did the tree wear to the pool party?
A: Swimming trunks!

Q: What kind of tree can fit into your hand?
A: A palm tree!

Q: What did the judge ask the dentist?
A: Do you swear to pull the tooth, the whole tooth and nothing but the tooth?

Q: When does a doctor get mad?
A: When he runs out of patients!

Q: Why was the broom late?
A: It over swept!

Q: What did one elevator say to the other elevator?
A: I think I'm coming down with something!

Q: Why did the cow cross the road?
A: To get to the udder side.

Q: What do you call a baby bear with no teeth?
A: A gummy bear!

Q: What do you call a pig who knows karate?
A: Pork chop!

Q: Where do fish keep their money?
A: In a river bank.

Q: What did one egg say to the other egg?
A: Let's get crackin'!

Q: Who did Frankenstein take to the dance?
A: His "ghoul" friend!

Q: Why is Superman's costume so tight?
A: Because he wears a size "S."

Q. What did one volcano say to the other?
A. I lava you.

Q. What do you get when you cross a cow and a duck?
A. Milk and quackers!

Q. What is an astronaut's favorite place on a computer?
A. The space bar!

Q. Why did the tomato blush?
A. Because it saw the salad dressing!

Q. What did the judge say when the skunk walked in the court room?
A. Odor in the court.

Q. Why don't skeletons fight each other?
A. They don't have the guts.

Q. Where do cows go for a vacation?
A. Moo York.

Q. Did you hear the joke about the roof?
A. Never mind, it's over your head!

Q: How do you close an envelope under water?
A: With a seal!

Q: How much does it cost a pirate to get earrings?
A: A buccaneer.

Q: What did one eye say to the other?
A: Between you and me, something smells.

Q: What did the one penny say to the other penny?
A: We make perfect cents.

Q: What do you call a story about a broken pencil?
A: Pointless!

Q: Who makes the best cake on a baseball team?
A: The batter.

Q: Why did the drum take a nap?
A: It was beat.

Q: What do envelopes say when you lick them?
A: Nothing. It shuts them up!

Q: What kind of room can you not go into?
A: A mushroom!

Q: Why did the student eat her homework?
A: Because the teacher said it was a piece of cake!

Q: Why did the boy throw a clock out the window?
A: To see time fly.

Q: What is a pirate's favorite treat?
A: Chips Ahoy!

Q: How do Vikings send secret messages?
A: Norse code.

Q: When do you go on red and stop on green?
A: When you are eating a watermelon.

Q: What do you call a fake noodle?
A: An impasta!

Q: Why do birds fly south in the winter?
A: Because it's too far to walk!

Q: What do you get if you cross a rabbit with an insect?
A: Bugs bunny.

Q: What does a baby computer call his father?
A: Data!

Q: What is a pretzel's favorite dance?
A: The Twist!

Q: What do witches put on their bagels?
A: Scream cheese.

Q: What part of a chicken is musical?
A: The drumstick!

Q: What kind of bow can't be tied?
A: A rainbow!

Q: What did the beaver say to the tree?
A: It's been nice gnawing you!

Q: Who made King Arthur's round table?
A: Sir Cumference!

Q: What is a ghosts favorite position in soccer?
A: Ghoul keeper.

Q: What is a snake's favorite subject?
A: Hiss-story.

Q: What does a cat say when somebody steps on its tail?
A: Me-Ow!

Q: What do you call a sleeping bull?
A: A bulldozer!

Q: What is the easiest way to count a herd of cattle?
A: With a cowculator.

Q: What do fish take to stay healthy?
A: Vitamin sea.

Q: What did the llama say when invited to a picnic?
A: Alpaca lunch!

Q: How can you tell if a hamburger was grilled in space?
A: It's a little meteor.

Q: What does a nosy pepper do?
A: Gets jalapeno business!

Q: What do you call an alligator wearing a vest?
A: An investigator!

Q: Where did the fish go when it needed an operation?
A: To the sturgeon.

Q: What is an astronaut's favorite meal?
A: Launch!

Q: What kind of birds stick together?
A: Vel-crows!

Q: What kind of music does a printer make?
A: A paper jam.

Q: How many tickles does it take to make a squid laugh?
A: Tentacles.

Q: What do you call two guys above a window?
A: Curt 'n Rod!

Q: What kind of cars do cows drive?
A: Cattle-acs!

Q: Want to hear a joke about pizza?
A: Never mind, it's too cheesy.

Q: What are caterpillars afraid of?
A: Dogerpillars!

Q: How do you turn soup into gold?
A: You add 24 carats!

Q: What do you call somebody with no body and no nose?
A: Nobody knows!

Q: Why couldn't the pony sing?
A: He was a little horse.

Q: What type of cheese lives under your bed?
A: Muenster.

Q: What did one plate say to the other plate?
A: Dinner's on me!

Q: Why did the bee go to the doctor?
A: Because he had hives!

Q: What did the tailpipe say to the muffler?
A: I'm exhausted.

Q: What kind of boats do smart people ride on?
A: Scholarships!

Q: What did the digital clock say to the grandfather clock?
A: Look grandpa, no hands!

Q: What kind of horses go out after dark?
A: Nightmares.

Q: What did the bunny say to the frog?
A: My name is Rabbit, not Ribbit!

Q: What do you get when you cross Bambi with a ghost?
A: Bamboo.

Q: What kind of streets do zombies like best?
A: Dead ends!

Q: What do you call a bear with no shoes on?
A: Barefoot!

Q: What do you call artificial spaghetti?
A: Mockaroni.

Q: What has more lives than a cat?
A: A frog because it croaks every night!

Q: What kind of bird does construction work?
A: A crane.

Q: Why did the man put wheels on his rocking chair?
A: He wanted to rock and roll!

Q: What do you say to a skeleton going on vacation?
A: Bone voyage!

Q: What happens to illegally parked frogs?
A: They get toad away!

Q: What did the alien say to the garden?
A: Take me to your weeder.

Q: What is a whale's favorite story?
A: The Humpback of Notre Dame.

Q: What do snowmen eat for breakfast?
A: Snowflakes!

Q: What do cats eat for breakfast?
A: Mice Krispies!

Q: What do you call a frightened scuba diver?
A: Chicken of the sea.

Q: What does a bee use to brush its hair?
A: A honeycomb.

Q: What did the mother broom say to the baby broom?
A: It's time to go to sweep!

Q: What is a vampire's favorite bank?
A: A blood bank!

Q: What did the hamburger name his daughter?
A: Patty!

Q: What did the tie say to the hat?
A: You go on ahead, I'll hang around!

Q: What do pigs write letters with?
A: Pig pens.

Q: What do you call a light bulb in a suit of armor?
A: A knight light!

Q: What do frogs like to drink?
A: Croak-a Cola!

Q: How does a lion like his steak cooked?

A: Medium roar!

Q: Why don't acrobats work in the winter?

A: They only do summer-saults.

Q: What do you call a crazy baker?

A: A dough-nut!

Q: Where does the Lone Ranger take his garbage?

A: To the dump, to the dump, to the dump, dump, dump!

Q: What did the worm ask the caterpillar?

A: Where'd you get that fur coat?

Q: Why does a giraffe have such a long neck?

A: Because its feet smell!

Q: What does Santa say when he walks backward?
A: Oh, oh, oh!

Q: What goes up but never comes down?
A: Your age.

Q: Why did the pear go out with the plum?
A: Because he couldn't find a date!

Q: How does Jack Frost travel?
A: By icicle.

Q: Why do fish live in salt water?
A: Because pepper makes them sneeze!

Q: Which state has the smallest sodas?
A: Mini-soda.

Q: What kind of music does a mountain like?
A: Rock music!

Q: What do you call a cow that gives no milk?
A: A milk dud...or an udder failure!

Q: What do you call an angry pea?
A: Grum-pea!

Q: Where was tennis invented?
A: Tennis-ee!

Q: What do you call a snail on a boat?
A: A snailor.

Q: Why can you never trust atoms?
A: Because they make up everything!

Q: What do you call an annoying vampire?
A: A pain in the neck.

Q: Where did the spaghetti go to dance?
A: The meat ball!

Q: Did you hear the story about the unsharpened pencil?
A: There's really no point to it.

Q: What lion never roars?
A: A dandelion!

Q: What's the best way to carve wood?
A: Whittle by whittle.

Q: What did the traffic light say to the car?
A: Don't look, I'm changing!

Q: What type of music do mummies like best?
A: Wrap music!

Q: Why did the rapper carry an umbrella?
A: Fo' drizzle!

Q: What do you do when you see a spaceman?
A: Park your car, man!

Q: What do you call a dinosaur who crashes his car?
A: A tyrannosaurus wrecks.

Q: Did you hear about the red ship and the blue ship that collided?
A: Both crews were marooned.

Q: Why did the pirate go to the Caribbean?
A: He wanted a little ARR and ARR!

Q: What do polar bears eat for dinner?
A: Iceberg-ers!

Q: What do you get when you cross a frog and a popsicle?
A: A hopsicle!

Q: What did the horse ask the waiter at the restaurant?
A: Where's my mane course?

Q: What's the worst vegetable to serve on a boat?
A: Leeks!

Q: What does a clam do on its birthday?
A: It shell-abrates!

Q: Why did the chicken cross the playground?
A: To get to the other slide.

Q: What's a crocodile's favorite game?

A: Snap!

Q: What happened when the dog went to the flea circus?

A: He stole the show!

Q: What do you give a sick horse?

A: Cough stirrup.

Q: How do you fix a cracked pumpkin?

A: With a pumpkin patch!

Q: What runs but does not walk?

A: Water.

Q: What's the best birthday present?

A: A broken drum. You can't beat it!

Q: What did the skunk say when the wind changed direction?
A: It's all coming back to me now!

Q: How do you take a pig to the hospital?
A: In a ham-bulance!

Q: What do you get when you cross a dinosaur and a pig?
A: Jurassic pork!

Q: What do you call a lost wolf?
A: A where wolf.

Q: What do robots like to eat?
A: Chips!

Q: Where do horses go when they are sick?
A: The horse-pital!

Q: How do mules open locked barn doors?
A: With don-keys!

Q: What do you call a rich elf?
A: Welfy.

Q: What is a snowman's favorite Mexican food?
A: Brrr-itos!

Q: What did the fisherman say to the magician?
A: Pick a cod, any cod.

Q: What do you call a vampire who cooks?
A: Count Spatula!

Q: Where do ants go on vacation?
A: Frants!

Q: Why don't cats like shopping online?
A: They prefer a cat-alog!

Q: What is the problem with twin witches?
A: You can never tell which witch is witch!

Q: What do you call a donkey with three legs?
A: A wonky.

Q: Where do snowmen make websites?
A: On the winternet!

Q: What do racing witches use to fly on?
A: Vroom sticks!

Q: What do you call an adventurous skeleton?
A: Indiana Bones.

Q: What does an aardvark like on its pizza?
A: ant-chovies!

Q: What do you call a dinosaur that doesn't take a bath?
A: A stinkasaurus.

Q: Where do pirates like to eat?
A: ARRby's!

Q: How does Darth Vader like his toast?
A: On the dark side.

Q: What kind of ship never sinks?
A: Friendship!

Q: What has a head and a tail but no body?
A: A coin!

Q: How do monsters start a fairy tale?
A: Once upon a slime...

Q: What does a shark eat with peanut butter?
A: Jellyfish!

Q: What did the beach say as the tide came in?
A: Long time, no sea!

Q: Why are chefs hard to like?
A: Because they beat the eggs, whip the cream, and mash the potatoes!

Q: What kind of bird is always out of breath?
A: A puffin.

Q: What do you call a rooster covered in chocolate?
A: Choc-o-doodle-doo!

Q: Why is Peter Pan always flying?
A: Because he can Neverland.

Q: Why did the football team go to the bank?
A: To get their quarterback!

Q: How do cats bake cakes?
A: From scratch.

Q: What do you call a fat jack-o-lantern?
A: A plumpkin!

Q: What kind of karate will make you sick?
A: Kung flu.

Q: What did the snake give to his wife before bed?
A: A good night hiss!

Q: What do you call a cow with a twitch?
A: Beef jerky!

Q: What do you get when you cross a pig with a cactus?
A: A porky-pine!

Q: How did the pirate get his ship so cheap?
A: It was on sail.

Q: What do you call a ghost's mother and father?
A: Transparents!

Q: What do you call a bee that won't make up its mind?
A: A may-bee.

Q: What planet is made out of fish?
A: Nep-tuna.

Q: Where do you catch a flying pig?
A: At the airpork!

Q: What do you call a fisherman who always makes mistakes?
A: Wrong John Silver.

Q: What's the hottest letter in the alphabet?
A: "B" because it makes oil...boil!

Q: What did one angel say to the other angel?
A: Halo.

Q: What do you call a unicorn with no horn?
A: A u-no-horn!

Q: What do you call octopus twins?
A: Itentacle twins.

Q: What happens when a cow does not shave?
A: He grows a moo-stache!

Q: What happens when you throw a green stone in the Red Sea?
A: It gets wet!

Q: What is a slug's favorite flavor of soda?
A: Lemon and slime.

Q: What did one fish say to the other at the party?
A: This party is off the hook!

Q: What's the best thing to have with you in the desert?
A: A thirst-aid kit!

Q: Why was the garbage sad?
A: Because it was down in the dumps.

Q: Where do funny frogs sit?
A: On silly pads!

Q: How long do chickens work?
A: Around the cluck.

Q: Why can't you believe a person who is sleeping?
A: Because they are lying!

Q: How do bees fly in the rain?
A: With their yellow jackets!

Q: How can you communicate with a fish?
A: Drop him a line.

Q: What do you call a cow spying on another cow?
A: A steak-out!

Q: Did you hear about the restaurant on the moon?
A: Great food, no atmosphere.

Q: Why are meteorologists always nervous?
A: Their future is always up in the air!

Q: Where did Noah keep his bees?
A: In the ark-hives.

Q: What is a mouse's favorite game?
A: Hide and squeak!

Q: What do you call a train transporting bubble gum?
A: A chew chew train.

Q: Why was the umbrella in a bad mood?
A: Because it was under the weather!

Q: Why was the artist in jail?
A: He had been framed!

Q: When does it rain money?
A: When there is change in the weather.

Q: What are the strongest days of the week?
A: Saturday and Sunday. Every other day is a weekday!

Q: What do cats like to eat with birthday cake?
A: Mice cream!

Q: Which monster makes the most jokes?
A: Prankenstein.

Q: What do you call a giant moose?
A: Enormoose!

27011013R00031

Made in the USA
San Bernardino, CA
07 December 2015